MW01506259

THE ULTIMATE 10
Natural Disasters

BLIZZARDS AND WINTER STORMS

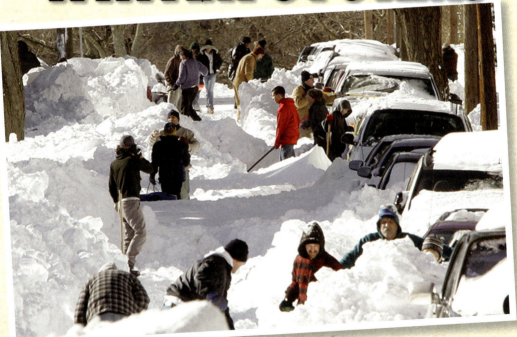

By Mark Stewart

Gareth Stevens
Publishing

Please visit our web site at **www.garethstevens.com**.
For a free catalog describing Gareth Stevens Publishing's list of high-quality books,
call 1-800-542-2595 (USA) or 1-800-387-3178 (Canada).
Gareth Stevens Publishing's fax: 1-877-542-2596

Library of Congress Cataloging-in-Publication Data available upon request from the publisher.
ISBN-13: 978-0-8368-9150-8 (lib. bdg.)
ISBN-10: 0-8368-9150-3 (lib. bdg.)

This edition first published in 2009 by
Gareth Stevens Publishing
A Weekly Reader® Company
1 Reader's Digest Rd.
Pleasantville, NY 10570-7000 USA

Senior Managing Editor: Lisa M. Herrington
Senior Editor: Brian Fitzgerald
Creative Director: Lisa Donovan
Senior Designer: Keith Plechaty
Photo Researcher: Charlene Pinckney
Special thanks to Barbara Bakowski, Amanda Hudson, Kristin Johnson, and Joann Jovinelly

Numbers of deaths and injuries from natural disasters vary from source to source, particularly for disasters that struck long ago. The figures included in this book are based on the best information available from the most reliable sources.

Picture credits:
Key: t = top, c = center, b = bottom
Cover, title page: Peter Pereira/New Bedford Standard Times/AP; pp. 4–5: John Cetrino/Getty Images; p. 7: (t) Bill Ross/AP, (b) Ron Frehm/AP; p. 8: Justin Sutcliffe/AP; p. 9 NASA; p. 11: (t) © Corbis, (b) AP; p. 12: (t) © Bettmann/Corbis, (b) AP; p. 13: (t) © Bettmann/Corbis, (b) Shutterstock; p. 15: © North Wind Picture Archives; p. 16: (t) Library of Congress, (b) Courtesy Gary O'Toole/opticphoto.net; p. 17: (t) © James L. Amos/Corbis, (b) Anne Chadwick Williams/Sacramento Bee/AP; p. 19: (t) Richard Corey/Getty Images, (b) Scott Olson/Getty Images; p. 20: Thomas Cheng/AFP/Getty Images; p. 21: (t) Jeff Kowalsky/AFP/Getty Images (both); p. 23: (t) Popperfoto/Getty Images, (b) © Bettmann/Corbis; p. 24: (t) AP, (b) © Galen Rowell/Corbis; p. 25: (t) © Jason Burke/Eye Ubiquitous/Corbis, (b) © George Steinmetz/Corbis; p. 27: AP; p. 28: The Herald Bulletin File/AP; p. 29: AP (2); p. 31: (t) Shutterstock, (b) © Scott Fischer/Woodfin Camp; p. 32: (t) Caroline Mackenzie/Woodfin Camp/Time Life Pictures/Getty Images, (b) Hiroyuki Kuraoka/AP; p. 33: (t) AP, (b) Binod Joshi/AP; p. 35: (t) Reuters; (b) © China Daily/Reuters; p. 36: (t) © Sean Yong/Reuters, (b) Imaginechina via AP Images; p. 37: Mark Ralston/AFP/Getty Images; p. 39: (t) © Troy Wayrynen/NewSport/Corbis, (b) © Bettmann/Corbis; p. 40: © Bettmann/Corbis; p. 41: (t) Newscom, (b) Charlie Neibergall/AP; p. 43: (t) Jim Beckel/The Oklahoman/AP, (b) Julie Smith/News Tribune/AP; p. 44: National Weather Service, Weather Underground/AP; p. 46: (t) NOAA, (c) Minnesota Historical Society, (b) David Duprey/AP.

All maps by Keith Plechaty

Printed in the United States of America

1 2 3 4 5 6 7 8 9 10 09 08

Table of Contents

Words in the glossary appear in **bold** type
the first time they are used in the text.

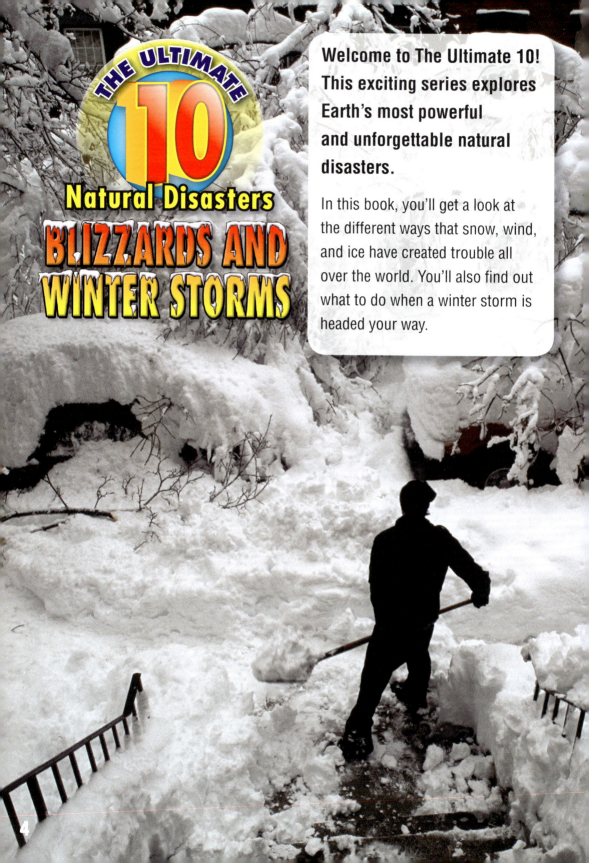

THE ULTIMATE 10

Natural Disasters

BLIZZARDS AND WINTER STORMS

Welcome to The Ultimate 10! This exciting series explores Earth's most powerful and unforgettable natural disasters.

In this book, you'll get a look at the different ways that snow, wind, and ice have created trouble all over the world. You'll also find out what to do when a winter storm is headed your way.

No force of nature can paralyze a huge area quite like a big winter storm, especially a **blizzard**. A blizzard is a dangerous mix of cold temperatures, howling winds, and steady snowfall. A blizzard includes winds of at least 35 miles (56 kilometers) per hour. The whirling snow prevents people from seeing more than a quarter mile ahead of them.

Blizzards and other wintry weather can shut down roads and businesses. They can trap people in their home or cars. The worst winter storms can even be deadly.

Brrrrr!

Here's a look at 10 of the most bone-chilling winter storms in history.

 The Superstorm, 1993

 The Great Blizzard, 1888

 The Donner Party Tragedy, 1846–1847

 New Year's Blizzard, 1999

 Terra Nova Expedition, 1911–1912

 Northeast Blizzard, 1978

 Mount Everest Disaster, 1996

 Chinese New Year's Blizzard, 2008

 The Great Serum Run, 1925

 Oklahoma Ice Storm, 2007

#1
The Superstorm of 1993
The Storm of the Century

What makes a winter storm a *superstorm*? Forecasters got their answer in March 1993. Three powerful weather systems joined forces near the Gulf of Mexico. The Superstorm stretched from Cuba to Canada. It covered the entire eastern third of the United States. Forecasters called it the Storm of the Century. Before it finally blew out to sea, the Superstorm took more than 300 lives.

FAST FACTS

The Superstorm of 1993

Location: Caribbean, eastern and central United States, and eastern Canada

Date: March 12–14, 1993

Impact: more than 300 killed, 2.5 million without power

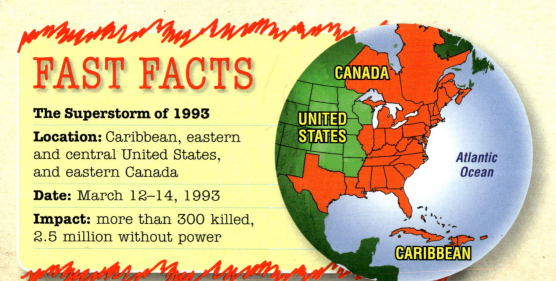

People all along the East Coast had to dig out after the 1993 Superstorm.

Wild Weather

Meteorologists predicted that the Superstorm would be historic—and they were right. Heavy snowfall is rare in the South, especially in March. Yet cities such as Birmingham, Alabama, were blanketed with more than a foot of snow. Winds faster than 100 miles (161 km) whipped across southern Florida. Along the coast, powerful waves swamped boats and drowned at least seven people. In other parts of the state, 15 tornadoes touched down.

A day later, much of the Northeast was buried in snow. On Long Island, New York, 18 homes were swept into the Atlantic Ocean. A freighter sank off the coast of Maine after reporting 100-foot (30-meter) waves. All 33 crew members were lost.

In Larchmont, New York, a woman climbed a snow mound to reach her buried car.

How a Snowstorm Forms

Storms form when two **air masses** collide. Most snowstorms in the United States form in the same way. A mass of cold, dry Arctic air meets a mass of warm, **humid** air from the Gulf of Mexico. The area where air masses meet is called a **front**. The moist air is pushed upward. When the moist air cools below 32° Fahrenheit (0° Celsius), snow falls to the ground.

SNOW

COLD AIR

WARM AIR

LAND

DIRECTION OF STORM

People in New York City climbed huge snowbanks after the Superstorm.

Collision Course

The Superstorm formed when snow and rain from the West Coast joined thunderstorms from the Gulf of Mexico. They clashed with a huge Arctic air mass. The result was one of the biggest storms anyone had ever seen.

Inside the Storm

The 1993 Superstorm showed the importance of predicting dangerous weather. One of the tools meteorologists use is **Doppler radar**. Doppler radar lets forecasters "look inside" storms. Doppler radar shows the strength and speed of a storm. It can also help forecasters predict how much snow will fall. Meteorologists saw that a "storm of the century" was on its way. Their warnings may have saved hundreds of lives.

Snowed In

Here's a look at the amount of snow the Superstorm dumped on some major cities:

City	Snowfall
Syracuse, NY	43 inches (109 cm*)
Albany, NY	27 inches (69 cm)
Pittsburgh, PA	25 inches (64 cm)
Chattanooga, TN	20 inches (51 cm)
Portland, ME	19 inches (48 cm)
Asheville, NC	19 inches (48 cm)
Washington, D.C.	13 inches (33 cm)

*cm = centimeters

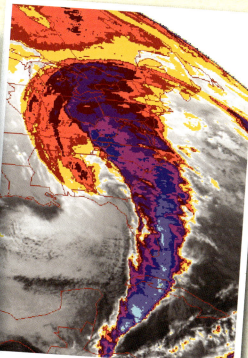

This Doppler radar image shows the huge area covered by the Superstorm.

Did You Know?

Every major airport on the East Coast closed at some point during the Superstorm. That had never happened before. All major highways north of Atlanta, Georgia, were also closed.

#2

The Great Blizzard of 1888
New York Under Cover

In March 1888, people in New York City were looking forward to a quiet spring. But on March 12, they awoke to a big surprise. Strong rains had changed to heavy snow. Howling winds reached 80 miles (129 km) per hour. Over the next few days, about a million people along the East Coast were trapped in their homes. Overall, more than 400 people died—half of them New Yorkers.

FAST FACTS

Great Blizzard of 1888

Location: Virginia to Maine

Date: March 11–14, 1888

Impact: More than 400 killed

UNITED STATES

Pacific Ocean

Atlantic Ocean

New York City streets were buried during the 1888 blizzard.

The Great White Hurricane

Days before the blizzard, temperatures along the East Coast were mild. Then the blizzard struck without warning. People from Maryland and Virginia to Maine were trapped. New York City was buried under more than 3 feet (91 cm) of snow. Strong winds created **snowdrifts** up to 50 feet (15 m) high. Telegraph and phone lines snapped. Communication was cut off. The strong blizzard became known as the Great White Hurricane.

Eyewitness

" I have run across passages in novels of great adventures in snow storms. I have always considered them exaggerations, but I shall never say so again. "

—Roscoe Conkling, a a New York City lawyer who died in the blizzard

This store awning in New York City was crushed by the weight of the snow.

Deadly Commute

The Great Blizzard stopped trains and trolleys. Streets were too dangerous for horse-drawn carriages. The only way to get to work was to walk. Some people were trapped in the snow and froze to death. Others got **frostbite** or fell ill.

Telegraph and telephone wires were knocked down by the snowy blast. Today, forecasters are much better at predicting major storms.

Spreading the Word

The first government weather agency was set up in 1870. At the time, weather news was sent by telegraph. There was no reliable way to warn people about approaching foul weather. Forecasters didn't monitor weather conditions round the clock, as they do today. On the night before the blizzard, forecasters decided that the storm was not a threat and went home. As a result, millions of people were caught off guard.

On the Right Track

In the late 1800s, people got around by railways and streetcars. After the blizzard, New Yorkers decided they needed an easier and faster way to travel. A few years later, plans began for a subway system. Above-ground electric and telegraph wires were also moved underground.

Construction of New York City's first electric-powered subway began in March 1900.

Did You Know?

New Yorkers depended on morning deliveries for their food. When the snow came, the deliveries stopped. That meant no milk. Parents feared their babies would starve. Many parents risked their lives in the deep snow to search for milk.

#3
The Donner Party Tragedy
Trapped in the High Sierras

In the 1840s, thousands of Americans moved west to build a new life. In April 1846, brothers Jacob and George Donner set out with their families from Illinois for Sutter's Fort, California. They joined a larger wagon train and reached the Sierra Nevada Mountains in late October. There, blizzards trapped the group for months. Nearly half of the 87 people didn't make it out alive.

FAST FACTS

The Donner Party Tragedy

Location: Sierra Nevada Mountains, California

Date: April 1846–April 1847

Impact: 41 killed

California

Sutter's Fort

Sierra Nevada Mountains

UNITED STATES

Atlantic Ocean

Pacific Ocean

This illustration shows what life may have been like for the trapped members of the Donner Party.

No Way Out

The Donner Party moved slowly through the Sierras. Heavy snowfall blocked their path. The group broke into two camps and waited for the bad weather to clear.

The mountain pass to California remained blocked. In mid-December, 15 people tried to walk through the pass on crude snowshoes. A month later, only seven of them reached Sutter's Fort. The rest had died. Four rescue parties set out to save the stranded settlers. The last survivors didn't reach the fort until April 29, 1847. In all, 41 members of the Donner Party died, including George and Jacob Donner.

Survival at Any Cost

Most members of the Donner Party died of starvation. The heavy snowfall kept them from getting food. They killed and ate their oxen and cattle. They soon had no choice but to eat bark and twigs. As members began to die off, the survivors did the unthinkable. Some ate the flesh of their dead companions. The snowshoers who struggled through the Sierras on foot also turned to cannibalism.

Snow was this high

Members of the Donner Party cut these trees to snow level. The height of the stumps shows the depth of the packed snow.

This monument stands in Donner Memorial State Park in California. Its base is 22 feet (6.7 m) high—the height of the snowdrifts of 1846–1847.

Drifting Away

The Donner Party could not move its wagons through the deep snowdrifts of the Sierras. Snowdrifts are huge mounds of snow created by wind. Even when snowfall is light, wind can blow snow into drifts several feet high. Near the campsite at what is now called Donner Lake, one snowdrift was estimated to be 22 feet (6.7 m) high!

Donner Pass in the Sierra Nevada Mountains is one of the snowiest places in the United States.

After the Tragedy

After the Donner Party tragedy, Californians created relief teams to help people through the mountains. They carried food and water to stranded settlers. The groups that later settled Salt Lake City, Utah, followed the trail cut by the Donner Party. The pass in the Sierras that was blocked is now called Donner Pass.

Did You Know?

When the first rescue party arrived, 8-year-old Patty Reed stayed behind to watch her 3-year-old brother, Thomas. He was too small to walk through the snowdrifts. When Patty finally arrived at Sutter's Fort, she was carrying a ragged doll (right). She had carried the doll with her all the way from Illinois. Patty lived to be 93 years old.

#4

New Year's Blizzard of 1999
The Party's Over

Late on January 1, 1999, snow flurries began to fall near the Great Lakes. A light snowfall seemed the perfect way to ring in 1999. By January 3, however, celebration had turned to disaster. Parts of the Midwest and eastern Canada were buried under nearly 2 feet (61 cm) of snow. When the snow stopped, record-low temperatures swept in. The blizzard was blamed for up to 100 deaths.

FAST FACTS

New Year's Blizzard of 1999

Location: Wisconsin, Illinois, Indiana, Michigan, Ohio, and Ontario, Canada

Date: January 1–3, 1999

Impact: Up to 100 killed

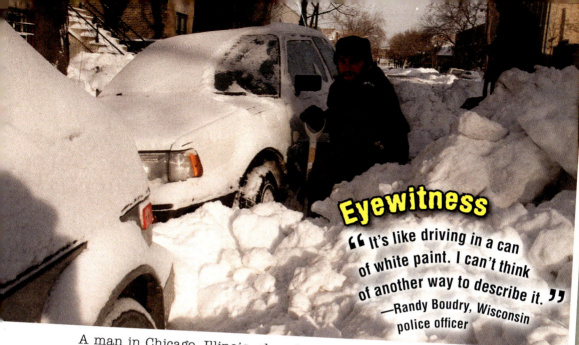

A man in Chicago, Illinois, shoveled his car out of the snow after the 1999 New Year's Blizzard.

Crippled Cities

Chicago is one of the world's busiest transportation centers. Its airports connect cities across the country. The New Year's Blizzard shut down the city's two major airports. More than 300,000 travelers were stranded. Freight trains moving through huge piles of snow fell behind schedule.

Airlines canceled flights in and out of Detroit, Michigan, too. The bad weather stopped bus service in Milwaukee, Wisconsin. In Indianapolis, Indiana, mail delivery was canceled.

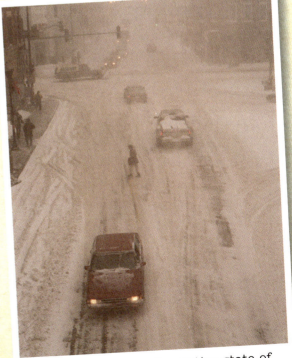

After the blizzard, the entire state of Illinois was declared a disaster area.

State of Emergency

Most Canadians are used to winter snowstorms. When the New Year's Blizzard blew across southern Ontario, however, the city of Toronto was overwhelmed. The mayor declared a state of emergency. The blizzard was followed by more snowstorms. More than 3 feet (1 m) of snow fell on Toronto in less than two weeks.

Canadian soldiers helped clear the streets of Toronto after the New Year's Blizzard.

Chilling Out

In the days after the New Year's Blizzard, temperatures dropped sharply. Temperatures were near 0° F (−18° C), but strong winds made it feel like −20° F (−29° C) or colder. That was because of the **windchill factor**. Windchill is a measure of the combined effect of wind and low temperature on the human body. Going outside on a very cold, windy day is extremely dangerous.

The Windchill Factor

Wind Speed	Air Temperature	Windchill Temperature	Effects on People
10 mph* (16 km/h)	0° F (−18° C)	−16° F (−27° C)	Bitter cold; ears, noses, cheeks, fingers, or toes may become numb.
30 mph (48 km/h)	0° F (−18° C)	−26° F (−32° C)	Bare skin freezes in 30 minutes.
55 mph (89 km/h)	0° F (−18° C)	−32° F (−36° C)	Bare skin freezes in 10 minutes.

*mph = miles per hour; km/h = kilometers per hour

A person walked down a snow-covered street in Detroit. The storm closed airports and stranded thousands of travelers in the city.

A Tale of Two Cities

The New Year's Blizzard pointed out the importance of being prepared for winter weather. Cities in the affected areas had not had such a severe snowstorm in two decades. Detroit took several days to dig out. More than 100,000 children were unable to return to school for a week.

Snowplows cleared highways in Detroit after the storm.

Chicago was better prepared for the heavy snow. By January 3, most of its streets had been cleared. Airports, buses, and trains were running on schedule. Schools were closed for only two days.

Did You Know?

Blood donors supply fresh blood to hospitals. After the New Year's Blizzard, people in the Midwest were unable to reach blood donation centers for up to a week. That led to a brief blood shortage in American hospitals.

#5
Terra Nova Expedition
Race to the South Pole

In 1910, Roald Amundsen and Robert Falcon Scott began one of the most famous races in history. Each wanted to become the first to reach the South Pole. Amundsen, of Norway, kept his plans secret. Scott, from England, announced his plans to the world before he boarded a ship called the *Terra Nova* bound for Antarctica. The race would bring one man world fame. A raging blizzard would cost the other his life.

FAST FACTS

Terra Nova Expedition

Location: Antarctica

Date: November 1, 1911– March 29, 1912

Impact: Five killed

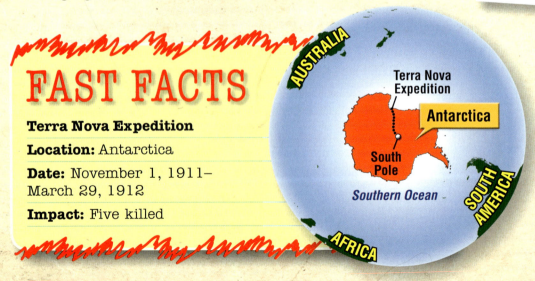

AUSTRALIA

Terra Nova Expedition

Antarctica

South Pole

Southern Ocean

AFRICA

SOUTH AMERICA

Too Late for Glory

The *Terra Nova* arrived in Antarctica on January 4, 1911. Scott and his party began a 1,766-mile (2,842-km) round trip to the South Pole in November 1911. They trudged through the snow and ice. The five-man team finally arrived at the South Pole on January 17, 1912. There, they found a Norwegian flag flapping in the wind. Amundsen had already been there. The team turned around to start the long walk back to their ship.

The *Terra Nova* sailed past icebergs as it made its way to Antarctica.

Eyewitness

❝ Outside the door of the tent it remains a scene of whirling drift. ... We shall stick it out to the end, but we are getting weaker. ... The end cannot be far. ❞

—Robert Falcon Scott's final diary entry

Norwegian flag

When Robert Falcon Scott (right) and his team reached the South Pole, they found a Norwegian flag. Roald Amundsen had made it there first.

The Long Road Home

Scott's party struggled to make it back to camp. They were exhausted from pulling heavy supply sleds. Injuries and frostbite slowed their progress. One man died in his sleep on February 17. A few weeks later, a second walked out of his tent in his socks. He was never seen again.

Scott (standing, center) and his four team members all died in the brutal weather of Antarctica.

Waiting for the End

A powerful blizzard trapped the remaining three men in their tent on March 20. The storm lasted for more than a week. The men were out of food and were freezing. Scott made a final diary entry on March 29. In November 1912, his body and those of the others were found in their tent.

The hut that Scott's team used as a base camp in Antarctica is still standing today.

At the Bottom of the World

Antarctica is the coldest place on Earth. In the Southern Hemisphere, the seasons are reversed. Scott's expedition took place during the Antarctic summer, when the Sun never sets. It was the warmest time of year at the South Pole. Yet the temperature never rose above 0° F (−18° C) during the journey.

Deadly Bites

All the men in Scott's party suffered from frostbite. This occurs when the nose, ears, fingers, or toes begin to freeze. Freezing kills the body's cells. The first sign of frostbite is a white color to the skin. Frostbite also deadens nerve endings, so victims do not feel anything. The skin turns brown or black. A frostbitten finger, toe, ear, or nose will eventually fall off. If left untreated, frostbite can be deadly.

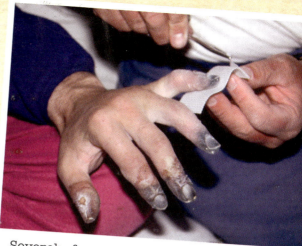

Severely frostbitten fingers will turn brown or black.

South Pole Survival

Today, the South Pole is home to researchers and scientists. They get special training to survive in freezing temperatures and heavy winds. Most blizzards in Antarctica do not produce much snowfall. Instead, strong winds push existing snow into the air.

Did You Know?

In Antarctica, the Sun shines 24 hours a day in summer (December). In winter (June), the Sun does not shine at all. The coldest temperature recorded at the South Pole was −128.6° F (−89.2° C) in July 1983.

#6
Northeast Blizzard of 1978
Worst Northeast Blizzard Since 1888

Two powerful weather systems collided over the northeastern United States in early February 1978. Cold air from the west crashed into warm, wet air moving up the Atlantic coast. The result was the worst blizzard in the Northeast since 1888. The blizzard packed winds of about 100 miles (161 km) per hour. The snow piled up, and the entire region shut down.

FAST FACTS

Northeast Blizzard of 1978

Location: New York, New Jersey, Connecticut, Rhode Island, Massachusetts, New Hampshire, Vermont, and Maine

Date: February 5–7, 1978

Impact: Up to 60 killed

People in Boston, Massachusetts, dug their cars out from snowdrifts following the February 1978 blizzard.

Deep Snow and High Tides

For 36 hours, people in New England watched the disaster build. Fierce winds blew snow, creating **whiteouts**. At times, snowfall reached 4 inches (10 cm) an hour. Powerful waves wiped out beach homes and flooded the coast. Thousands of people fled to shelters as snowdrifts climbed to 15 feet (5 m). Power outages were widespread. Boston, Massachusetts, and Providence, Rhode Island, were buried under 27 inches (69 cm) of snow. People needed a week to dig out from the mess. President Jimmy Carter declared parts of the region federal disaster areas.

" I've never seen such a mess. As soon as this is over, I'm moving inland! "
—Doug Call, New England resident

Triple Trouble

The Northeast Blizzard of 1978 was the third major storm to hit early in the year. In mid-January, heavy snow fell on parts of New England. A few days later, a blizzard dumped several feet of snow in Ohio, Illinois, Indiana, Kentucky, Michigan, and Wisconsin. High winds created 25-foot (8-m) snowdrifts. Windchill temperatures dropped to –60° F (–51° C) in some places. Thousands of people were stranded in their cars and homes. More than 160 people died during these extreme winter events.

A stranded driver walked to a closed gas station after the January 1978 blizzard hit Daleville, Indiana.

Nor'easters can bring heavy snow or rain to the eastern United States.

Nor'easters

The storm that provided the moisture for the Northeast Blizzard was a **nor'easter**. During a nor'easter, winds blow warm, moist air inland from over the Atlantic Ocean. The winds spin counterclockwise as the storm moves up the east coast. Meanwhile, cold air from Canada moves south along the Atlantic coast. This combination brings heavy rain or snow and coastal flooding to the Northeast.

Cars and trucks were stranded in deep snow along the highway in Dedham, Massachusetts.

Havoc on the Highways

After the Northeast Blizzard ended, the cleanup took much longer than expected. A big problem was getting the highways moving again. Thousands of cars were stranded on major roadways across southern New England, New York, and New Jersey. Many drivers set out on foot to look for shelter. Some who chose to stay paid a high price. When snow blocked their tailpipes, the exhaust came into the car and killed them.

After the blizzard, rescue workers searched for people trapped inside stranded cars.

Did You Know?

The blizzard affected every type of business. For the first time in 106 years, *The Boston Globe* newspaper wasn't delivered to customers.

#7

1996 Mount Everest Disaster
Tragedy on Top of the World

Mount Everest towers 29,035 feet (8,850 km) above sea level. It is in the Himalayas, on the border between China and Nepal. More than 2,000 people have climbed to the top. More than 200 others have died trying. Sudden storms often trap climbers. In May 1996, three groups reached the top of Everest from Nepal. On their way down, they battled a deadly blizzard for 16 terrifying hours.

FAST FACTS

1996 Everest Disaster

Location: Mount Everest, on the border of Nepal and China

Date: May 10–11, 1996

Impact: Five killed

ASIA

Nepal   China

Mount Everest

Indian Ocean

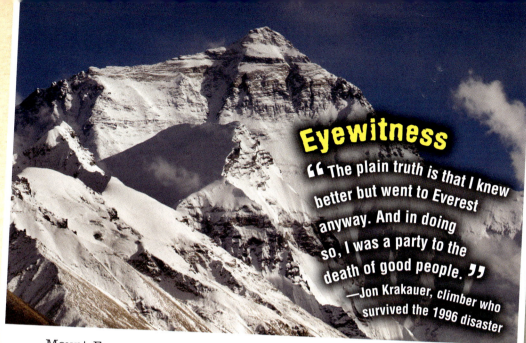

Mount Everest in Asia is the tallest mountain on Earth.

A Late Start

The trek up Mount Everest takes several weeks, with stops at four camps. The final leg of the climb starts at 25,900 feet (7,894 m). It must be done quickly. Up high, there is less oxygen in the air. People can become ill.

The three groups were delayed from the start of their climb on May 10. Guides had not set the climbing ropes. At 3 P.M., several climbers were still struggling to the top. To get back to camp safely, a climber should reach the **summit** by 2 P.M., experts say. As the groups reached

Climbers waited to reach the summit on May 10, 1996. This photo was taken by Scott Fischer, a guide who died hours later.

the top, snow began to fall. The storm became a blizzard with fierce winds of 70 miles (113 km) per hour. The lines and trails for the climb down were soon buried under ice and snow.

Trapped on Everest

The blizzard lasted until midnight. The climbers and their guides became lost or stranded. Many were injured and frostbitten. All had run out of bottled oxygen. Several were freezing to death. A few made it back to camp during the storm. Others came close but were blinded by the snow and had to stop. The next morning, rescuers found five bodies on the mountain, including two guides. Their deaths proved that no one is safe when a blizzard hits Everest.

Several climbers in this 1996 expedition group died on Mount Everest.

Many climbers on Everest wear special oxygen masks to help them breathe.

Thin Air

Every second counts for climbers on Mount Everest. At **altitudes** above 25,000 feet (7,620 m), there is less oxygen in the **atmosphere**. A lack of oxygen can cause the mind and body to shut down. In the May 1996 blizzard, weather conditions caused oxygen levels to drop by an extra 14 percent.

Eyewitness

❝ Above 26,000 feet [7,925 m], there's just not much one person can do for another. ❞
—Jon Krakauer

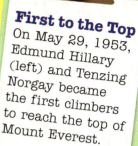

Crowded Mountain

After the 1996 disaster, people argued about who should be allowed to climb Everest. In recent years, mountain climbing has become more popular. Equipment has improved, too. As a result, the number of inexperienced climbers on Everest has increased. This trend is dangerous. From 1953 to 1973, there was less than one death per year on Everest. By 2007, the number had reached six per year.

Did You Know?

The most amazing story of survival was that of climber Beck Weathers. Blinded by high altitude, he was left for dead. He suffered frostbite and then slipped into a coma. Everyone was amazed when Weathers later regained **consciousness** and stumbled into camp!

#8
Chinese New Year's Blizzard
Stranded for the Holidays

There is never a good time for a winter storm. Yet no time could be worse for wintry weather than during the holidays. People in China learned that lesson the hard way in 2008. February 7 was the Lunar New Year, China's most important holiday. Millions of people planned to travel to be with their families. Instead, much of the country ended up paralyzed by four weeks of snow and ice.

FAST FACTS

Chinese New Year's Blizzard

Location: Southern China

Date: January–February 2008

Impact: More than 100 killed, nearly 200 million stranded

ASIA

China

Indian Ocean

People waited to buy train tickets in southeastern China. They held umbrellas to shield themselves from the snow.

Unhappy New Year

China is a huge country with many different **climates**. Northern China is famous for its frigid winters, but southern China almost never sees snow. A week before the Lunar New Year, snow and ice blanketed the southern provinces. Power lines were destroyed, and rail lines were snowed under. Highways iced over, and airplanes were grounded. One in eight people was stranded.

A worker shoveled snow from the collapsed roof of a car showroom in southern China.

Where Do We Go From Here?

Millions of people crammed into train and bus stations. Those who were able to start their journeys home soon found themselves stuck in remote areas. Cars and buses skidded on the ice or ran out of fuel in long traffic jams. Trains sat motionless on the tracks, unable to move in either direction.

Whether on foot or in cars, travelers in southern China moved very slowly during the 2008 blizzard.

After several days, the Chinese government suggested that everyone forget about going home for the holidays. The storms did not let up until February 6. By then, it was too late.

Snow Removal

Southern China does not have the snowplows and other machines needed to remove large amounts of snow. In fact, there are very few snow shovels in that part of the country. Soldiers were called in to help shovel snow.

Maximum Impact

Heavy snow in southern China did much more than ruin people's travel plans. It created a hardship that was felt by millions of people. Much of China's food comes from the region. Winter weather destroyed countless acres of crops and prevented tons of food from reaching major Chinese cities. Prices of basic foods rose sharply. A coal shortage in China grew worse. Power plants depend on coal, so many had to shut down. People spent the Lunar New Year without electricity or heat. In all, the snowstorm of 2008 cost the Chinese people more than $4 billion.

An airport worker removed snow and ice from an airplane in Shanghai, China.

Did You Know?

Blizzards can occur at any time of the year. One of China's worst came during the summer of 1989, in the country's remote western region. More than 60 people died during storms in June and July of that year.

#9
The Great Serum Run
Birth of the Iditarod

Diphtheria is a disease spread by coughing and sneezing. Without treatment, it can be deadly to children. In January 1925, Curtis Welch was the lone doctor in Nome, Alaska. When diphtheria broke out there, he was helpless to stop its spread. He did not have the serum, or medicine, he needed to treat the illness. The race to save the children of Nome made a sled dog named Balto world famous.

FAST FACTS

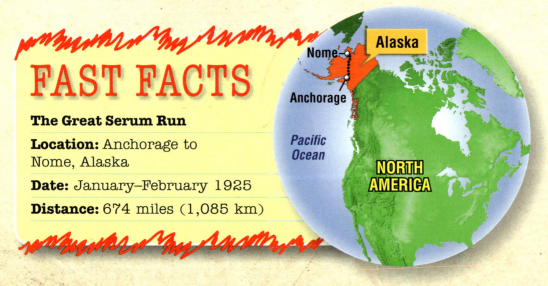

The Great Serum Run

Location: Anchorage to Nome, Alaska

Date: January–February 1925

Distance: 674 miles (1,085 km)

Alaska

Nome

Anchorage

Pacific Ocean

NORTH AMERICA

Dogsled teams in Alaska often face harsh weather conditions.

A Call for Help

Dr. Welch radioed for help. The nearest supply of medicine was in Anchorage. That city is almost 1,000 miles (1,609 km) from Nome. The supplies were sent partway by train. The last 674 miles (1,085 km) of the trip to Nome, however, would have to be made by dogsled.

Brave Balto

The plan was for 20 drivers and their dogsled teams to run a relay to Nome. As the first team hit the trail, a blinding blizzard started.

Gunnar Kasson is shown here with his famous dog Balto.

Temperatures dropped to –50° F (–46° C). On February 1, Gunnar Kasson set out on the next-to-last leg. A husky named Balto led Kasson's team of dogs through the blizzard.

Gunnar Kasson posed with his sled dog team. Balto is by his side.

Wild Night

At times, the snow was so heavy that Kasson could not see his dogs. Unable to find the last team, he drove the final 25 miles (40 km) to Nome. During the night, fierce winds blew Kasson's sled over. Somehow, Balto was able to stay on the trail. He saved the team from plunging into a river. On February 2, Kasson entered Nome to cheering crowds. He delivered the medicine to Dr. Welch, and the diphtheria outbreak ended. Kasson and Balto became national celebrities.

A Dog's Life

Kasson later sold Balto and his team to a traveling show. The dogs became very unhealthy. In 1927, a man named George Kimble raised $2,300 from Ohio schoolchildren to buy the famous team. They lived out their lives in a special exhibit at the Cleveland Zoo.

Eyewitness

" I couldn't see the trail. Many times I couldn't even see my dogs, so blinding was the [snow]. I gave Balto, my lead dog, his head and trusted him. ... The credit is his. " —Gunnar Kasson

The Great Race

The popular Iditarod Trail Sled Dog Race follows the route of the famous Serum Run. The Iditarod began in 1973. Mushers and their teams often face the same terrible weather that Kasson and Balto did. Teams can take from eight days to two weeks to complete the 1,161-mile (1,868-km) course, depending on the weather.

Jeff King won the Iditarod Trail Sled Dog Race four times from 1993 to 2006.

Whiteout!

On his way to Nome, Kasson experienced a whiteout. In a whiteout, snowfall is so heavy that a person can only see things a few feet away. Sometimes it is impossible to tell where the ground ends and the air begins.

Driving during whiteout conditions can be very dangerous.

Did You Know?

The worldwide publicity received by Balto helped make the diphtheria vaccination popular. In the early 1920s, the disease killed about 10,000 children a year. Today, it is almost unknown.

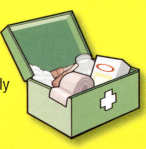

#10

Oklahoma Ice Storm of 2007
Frozen in Time

When a winter storm is coming, people worry about how much snow will fall. They should worry even more about ice. The people of Oklahoma know this all too well. Ice storms are common in the state. In December 2007, nearly 1 million homes lost power. The state's two largest cities, Tulsa and Oklahoma City, were covered in ice. The ice storm also affected people in other states, from Kansas to Michigan.

FAST FACTS

Oklahoma Ice Storm of 2007

Location: Oklahoma and seven other states

Date: December 8–10, 2007

Impact: At least 27 killed

UNITED STATES

Pacific Ocean

Atlantic Ocean

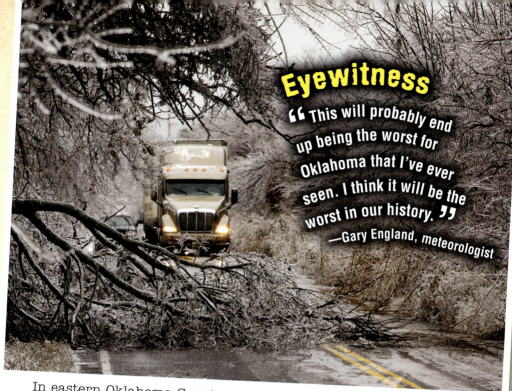

In eastern Oklahoma County, cars and trucks could not pass through roads where tree limbs had fallen.

Heavy Damage

During the 2007 storm, **freezing rain** fell for parts of three days. When the rain stopped, much of Oklahoma was coated with up to 1.5 inches (3.8 cm) of ice. The added weight of the ice brought down miles of phone and electric lines. More lines came down as tree branches snapped above them. Soon, one in three Oklahomans was in the dark. With the roads iced over, repair crews were unable to get to many homes. Thousands of people fled to temporary shelters.

Fallen branches damaged this car in Jefferson City, Missouri. Entire trees were uprooted by the storm.

Icy Emergency

Outside Oklahoma, nearly 1 million people lost power. States of emergency were declared in Kansas and Missouri. The ice storm led to at least 27 deaths. Most were in traffic accidents on icy roads.

How Ice Storms Form

Ice storms happen when the ground is colder than the air above it.

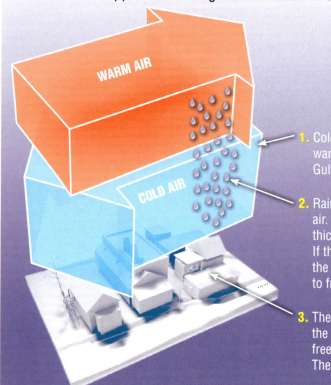

WARM AIR

COLD AIR

1. Cold Arctic air slides under warmer moist air from the Gulf of Mexico.

2. Rain falls through the cold air. If the layer of cold air is thick, the rain turns to **sleet**. If the cold layer is very shallow, the rain does not have a chance to freeze.

3. The rain strikes objects on the ground that are below the freezing point of 32° F (0° C). The water instantly freezes.

Did You Know?

During a storm like the one that hit Oklahoma, more than 500 pounds (227 kilograms) of ice can form on telephone wires. Ice storms are also destructive to wildlife. Birds have been known to freeze to their branches. Small mammals have had their paws freeze to the ground.

Be Prepared!

Meteorologists can predict winter storms more accurately than ever. Here's how to stay safe:

Before a Winter Storm

☑ Pay close attention to weather reports.

☑ Put together a disaster emergency kit. It should include canned food, several gallons of water per person, a flashlight, batteries, and a radio. Also include plenty of warm clothing, blankets, and waterproof boots for each family member.

☑ Create a storm emergency plan. Locate your nearest public shelter in the event of an evacuation. Keep a list of important phone numbers handy.

☑ If your home is drafty, cover windows with clear plastic.

During a Winter Storm

☑ Stay indoors! Stay tuned to TV and radio broadcasts for updated weather conditions.

☑ If you are stuck outside, stay in your car with the engine off or seek warm shelter.

After a Winter Storm

☑ Listen to the radio for warnings and information about road conditions. Roads and sidewalks may still be covered with ice and snow.

☑ Before going outside, dress warmly. Wear waterproof boots, a hat, and gloves. A scarf worn over the mouth can help protect lungs from cold air. Do not stay outside for long periods.

☑ Watch out for fallen power lines.

Source: American Red Cross

Honorable Mentions

Knickerbocker Storm

January 27–29, 1922

In late January 1922, Washington, D.C., was hit by a major blizzard. The roof of the Knickerbocker Theater collapsed under 28 inches (71 cm) of snow. The theater was the largest movie house in the city. Nearly 100 people died, and more than 130 others were injured.

Armistice Day Blizzard

November 11–12, 1940

November 11, 1940, marked the 22nd anniversary of the end of World War I. From Texas to Michigan, the parades and parties ended early. It was 60° F (15° C) in the morning, but by noon, it was snowing. By the end of the next day, more than 2 feet (61 cm) of snow buried much of the Midwest. More than 150 people died.

Buffalo Blizzard of 2001

December 24–28, 2001

Buffalo, New York, is famous for its snowstorms. Cold temperatures and moisture from the Great Lakes mix to produce huge amounts of snow. A December 2001 storm broke records in America's snow capital. More than 6 feet (183 cm) fell in less than a week!

Glossary

air mass: a large body of air with the same temperature and humidity

altitudes: heights of objects above sea level

atmosphere: the thick layer of air that surrounds Earth

blizzard: a dangerous mix of cold temperatures, strong winds, and steady snowfall

climates: the average weather in areas over a long period of time

consciousness: the natural state of being awake and aware

Doppler radar: a special kind of radar that measures wind direction and speed

freezing rain: very cold rain that falls to the ground and instantly freezes

front: the area where air masses meet

frostbite: a skin condition caused by freezing temperatures

humid: air that contains a lot of moisture

meteorologists: scientists who study Earth's climate and weather

nor'easter: a heavy rain or snowstorm in the Northeast that combines warm air from the Atlantic Ocean and cold air from Canada and that usually causes flooding

sleet: a cold, slushy substance halfway between rain and snow

snowdrifts: huge mounds of snow created by wind

summit: the highest point on a mountain

whiteouts: conditions that occur during heavy snowfalls that make it hard to see

windchill factor: a measure of the combined effect of wind and low temperature on the human body

For More Information

Books

Allen, Jean. *Blizzards* (Natural Disasters). Mankato, Minn.: Capstone Press, 2003.

Ball, Jacqueline A. *Blizzard! The 1888 Whiteout* (X-Treme Disasters That Changed America). New York: Bearport Publishing, 2005.

Pipe, Jim. *Earth's Weather and Climate* (Planet Earth). Pleasantville, N.Y.: Gareth Stevens, 2008.

Web Sites

Celebrate Boston—The Blizzard of 1888
www.celebrateboston.com/disasters/storms/blizzardof1888.htm

NOAA: Storm of the Century
celebrating200years.noaa.gov/events/storm/welcome.html

Publisher's note to educators and parents: Our editors have carefully reviewed these web sites to ensure that they are suitable for children. Many web sites change frequently, however, and we cannot guarantee that a site's future contents will continue to meet our high standards of quality and educational value. Be advised that children should be closely supervised whenever they access the Internet.

Index

About the Author

When Mark Stewart was growing up in New York City, he listened wide-eyed as his grandmother described the Blizzard of 1888. Ever since, Mark has loved to read and write about winter weather. If it's snowing, Mark will shovel off his driveway while his daughters, Rachel and Mariah, stay warm inside their home in Monmouth Hills, New Jersey.